OUTDOOR LIFE

essential

DEER HUNTING

for teens

Jonathan Ceaser

HIGH
interest
books

Children's Press
A Division of Grolier Publishing
New York / London / Hong Kong / Sydney
Danbury, Connecticut

To my mom

Book Design: Nelson Sa

Photo Credits: Cover © Index Stock Photography, Inc.; p. 5 © D. Robert Franz/Corbis; pp. 6, 9 © Raymond Gehman/Corbis; p.11 © D. Robert Franz/Corbis; p. 12 © Lynda Richardson/Corbis; p. 14 © Raymond Gehman/Corbis;p. 17 © Index Stock Photography, Inc.; pp. 20, 23, 25, 27, 28, 31, 32, 35, 39 © Raymond Gehman/Corbis; p. 40 © David Turnley/Corbis.

Cataloging-in-Publication Data

Ceaser, Jonathan.
   Essential deer hunting for teens / by Jonathan Ceaser.
      p. cm. – (Outdoor life)
   Includes bibliographical references and index.
   Summary: This book presents information about deer hunting, including the equipment needed, where to hunt, when to hunt, and safety tips.
   ISBN 0-516-23354-8 (lib. bdg.) – ISBN 0-516-23554-0 (pbk.)
   1. White-tailed deer hunting—Juvenile literature
   2. Deer hunting for teenagers—Juvenile literature [1. Hunting] I. Title. II. Series.
   SK301.C4 2000
00-022641
   799.2'7652—dc21

CONTENTS

INTRODUCTION

For ancient people, hunting was a way of life. They needed to follow herds of game (animals hunted for sport or food) for survival. Humans used animal furs for clothing. They used animal bones, horns, and hooves to make tools. In more advanced cultures, people began to hunt for sport. When hand-held firearms were invented, hunting for sport became even more popular.

Today, the white-tailed deer is one of the most popular targets for hunters in North America. The whitetail is found in almost every state in the United States, as well as in several parts of Canada and Mexico. Each year, millions of hunters of all ages take to the woods and plains across North America to hunt the whitetail. Many young people hunt with their families or friends. It gives them a chance to bond with each other. It also gives them a chance to learn about nature and about a proud, beautiful animal.

The white-tailed deer, or whitetail,
is a popular target for hunters.

1
HUNTING METHODS

Many hunters choose to hunt deer with firearms.

The two methods by which deer are hunted are with a firearm or a bow and arrow. Hunting with a bow and arrow is referred to as bow hunting. Most experts agree that bow hunting requires more experience and practice than does hunting with firearms. However, firearms can be very dangerous, so it is important that you follow firearm safety rules.

TYPES OF FIREARMS

Hunting firearms include rifles and shotguns. A rifle has spiral grooves in its barrel. The grooves make bullets spin as they are shot. Shotgun barrels are ungrooved. Shotguns fire buckshot pellets that spread out toward the target. Most beginning hunters use shotguns. Have a sales clerk help you when you go to buy a hunting firearm.

BUYING A GUN

The laws for buying guns vary from state to state. In most cases, there are restrictions on the age of gun buyers. Your parent or guardian will probably have to buy the weapon and register it under his or her own name. Some counties also have laws that say which types of firearms a person can buy. In some counties, hunters may only use shotguns. This law exists in many places with flat land, where a bullet from a rifle could carry too far and hit someone.

Shotguns can be purchased in 10-, 12-, 16-, or 20-gauge size. The gauge is the number of lead balls that just fit inside a rifle's barrel. The smaller the gauge number, the bigger the barrel. The most affordable and popular shotgun for whitetail deer hunting is the 12-gauge.

There are several basic models of rifles. The model you choose will depend on the terrain

The rifle is a popular weapon for deer hunters.

where you hunt. Bolt-action (loaded with a hand-operated bolt), high-powered rifles normally have very good scopes. These scopes help give you long-range accuracy. You use them in wide-open spaces. Smaller caliber

weapons are less powerful and accurate, but they are not as heavy. These rifles are easier to carry when you hunt in thick forests, or when you have to move around when you hunt.

Know Your Weapon

No matter which weapon you choose, you must learn everything about it before you enter the woods. Read the instruction manual and warning pamphlets that come with the gun. Always have an experienced adult teach you how to use the weapon. Then go to a firing range and practice using your weapon.

USING YOUR FIREARM

Always keep the weapon on safety until you are ready to fire it. Find the right range from your target. Then stand or sit in a relaxed position. Bring the stock of the gun to your shoulder, switch the safety off, and aim at the target. Slowly exhale. Hold your breath. Then gently squeeze the trigger.

A scope helps the hunter aim from a long distance away from his or her target.

Scope vs. No Scope

If you use a scope, go to a shooting range or to private property that you have permission to use. Set the scope's range for a distance of 100 yards (91 m). To do this, place a paper target 100 yards away. Fire three rounds at the target. Then, go check where the rounds hit the target. Where the shots are grouped will tell you how much the scope should be adjusted. Your scope will have separate adjustment dials on it to help you aim. You should adjust the dials until you can fire three shots within the center of the target.

If you use a shotgun or an open-sighted (without a scope) rifle, you need more practice to hit targets. Make sure you feel totally comfortable with your weapon. When you have a solid amount of practice under your belt and all of your gear prepared, you are almost ready to begin the hunt.

BOW HUNTING

Hunting Tip

If your shot hits a deer, make note of two things: where the deer was when you shot, and the last place you saw the deer after you shot. This will help you to find the deer if it runs away.

Some experienced hunters prefer to use a bow and arrow to hunt deer. Many people feel bow hunting is fairer than hunting with a firearm. (It is harder to hit a deer with a bow and arrow, so the deer has more of a chance of getting away.) Some people also like to hunt as people did before firearms were invented.

Modern hunters use a bow that is made of wood, fiberglass, and glue. This is called a compound bow. Today's compound bows have strings and pulleys that give the arrow more speed. The string of a compound bow is made of nylon. Modern arrows are made of aluminum or fiberglass, with steel points and plastic fins.

Many experienced hunters like to bow hunt for deer.

2
DEER-HUNTING GEAR

Hunters wear hats and layer
their clothing to stay warm.

It's important that you have the right gear, including appropriate clothing, a pack, and compass, before you begin hunting.

Hunting season takes place during cold months, usually in the late fall and winter. To avoid exposure to the cold, you will want to layer your clothing. Start with a layer made of polyester, silk, or wool. These fabrics allow moisture to evaporate while keeping you warm and dry. Do not wear all-cotton clothes next to your skin. If you get wet (from the rain or from sweating), the cotton will trap the moisture. This will make it difficult for your skin to dry off and warm up.

Good boots are a must. They should be sturdy and waterproof. A hat and gloves are also necessary. You may want to keep your face warm by wearing a ski mask. You also should wear soft fabrics. Soft-fabric clothing does not make as much noise when you walk through the woods.

Also, many hunters like to wear camouflage clothing. Camouflage clothing helps you blend into the woods. The white-tailed deer is color-blind. However, they do see patterns very well. If you wear camouflage clothing, these deer will have a very difficult time seeing you.

COVERING YOUR BODY ODOR

A deer's sense of smell is very powerful. For this reason, you must make sure that your clothing and body are completely free of scent. Scent will make a deer aware of a hunter's presence.

To hunt successfully, you will need to cover your body odor. Check your local sporting goods store for special body soap, shampoo, and deodorant that get rid of odors. Also, keep in mind that a deer easily can smell body

Your deer-hunting gear should include a warm hat, clothing marked with orange, and a pack.

sweat. You should not wear heavy clothing that will make you sweat. You also may want to spray a cover scent on your clothing and boots before you enter the woods. Finally, always wear gloves while going to your hunting site. The skin on your hands gives off oils that a deer can smell.

MAINTAINING YOUR CLOTHING

Every piece of clothing must be descented with special odor-killing detergent. There are several types on the market.

After you wash your clothing, hang it on a line outside to dry. Machine dryers contain scents from detergents and fabric softeners that a deer can instantly detect. After the clothing is dry, place your clothes in a plastic bag or container. Put a few dry leaves and pine needles in with the clothes. Then, when you wear these clothes, you will smell like a deer's natural surroundings.

Being Seen

Remember, you don't want deer to see you, but you do want other hunters to see you. Make sure to wear something that is colored bright orange, such as a hat or vest. In most states, hunters must wear some article of blaze orange clothing. Even if your state doesn't have a law, bright orange clothing will help other hunters to see you. If other hunters see this color, they will know you are not a deer!

PACK

You will need a pack when you go hunting. It should contain hunting licenses and tags, rope, a map and compass, water and food, a hunting knife, a flashlight, and extra clothes. Licenses and tags must be bought before the hunt. They are necessary to legally register any harvested animal. A harvested animal is one that you have shot and recovered. Many states require that you take a short safety course before you can get a hunting license.

3
WHERE TO HUNT

Joining a hunting club can be a
good way to meet other hunters.

Depending on where you live, finding good places to hunt can be difficult. Most states have public wildlife areas that are set aside for hunting. State wildlife departments have detailed maps of these areas. Game officials often will offer good advice about places to hunt.

Another good idea is to find friends or family that will allow you to hunt on their private land. Private land is usually more safe than public land. There are fewer hunters on private land.

HUNTING CLUBS

You also can join a hunting club. These organizations have private land set aside for their use only. Hunting clubs can be a fun way to meet new people. You also can learn valuable tips from more experienced sportsmen. Some clubs sponsor special groups for beginning hunters. Ask your local hunting dealer for information about these programs.

BE A SCOUT!

No matter which piece of land you decide to hunt on, you should scout it out before the season begins. Walk the land using a map and compass while taking important notes of any good hunting spots. Most importantly, you should remember any feeding areas. These most commonly are fields of corn, wheat, or beans, groups of oak or beechnut trees, and fruit tree orchards.

TRAILS

Deer use specific trails every day to enter and exit for feeding. Once you have discovered these trails, check to see which ones are the most heavily used. The trails with the most (and deepest) footprints, and with the most droppings, are the best trails to hunt. If these

Hunters should get to know the land where they are going to hunt.

paths cross each other, it shows that animals interact at these places. These are great spots to find animals. Areas with water, such as a pond or spring, often have similar trails.

When you find a trail, stay a couple of feet away and follow it to an area with thicker plant growth. These most often are bedding (sleeping) areas. Deer sleep during the day and feed mainly at night. They may be startled by your presence in a bedding area. If you notice several deer leap away, remain calm. Carefully walk in the direction from which you originally came. You don't want to scare the deer into moving to another bedding area.

On hills or mountains, most deer will move along trails near the edge. Their senses of sight, hearing, and smell are enhanced when they are looking down at objects. Watch the deer at daybreak and in the afternoon. Notice their movements. This may help you bag a nice deer on opening day.

TREE STANDS

Some hunters like to build places in trees where they can sit and wait for deer. These places are called tree stands. Tree stands allow the hunter to see more deer without them seeing the hunter. Tree stands also keep a hunter's scent above the deer's nose. In fact, deer often walk right under a hunter's stand. There may already be existing stands where you hunt. If not, ask the landowners if you can build a permanent tree stand. Build them in trees that are within range of the hunting areas.

Tree stands help hunters to scout deer without being seen.

Deer often hunt for food around berry bushes, grapevines, and old orchards. Deer are especially drawn to acorn trees.

Be extremely careful when building fixed tree stands. They must be constructed of sturdy wood and large nails or bolts to hold your weight. Always use extreme caution when entering and exiting a stand. Use a safety strap that will hold you in the tree if you fall.

Most important, use a rope to pull your weapon up to you in the tree. Always make sure it is unloaded and that the safety switch is on. Many accidents occur each year that could be avoided if people just followed these simple rules.

If hunting on public land, you may want to look into the use of a portable stand, which you can carry and move. A portable stand allows the hunter to climb a tree in a matter of minutes. Several models are available at sports stores. Ask a clerk to show you how to use one.

This hunter has a good view from high in his tree stand.

4
WHEN TO HUNT

Deer tend to move a lot
while they are looking for food.

Deer behave differently during the fall and winter, when the male deer try to mate with female deer. The mating period is called the rut. Deer's behavior changes during three periods: the prerut, the rut, and the postrut.

PRERUT

The prerut, in early fall, is an excellent time to spot deer while they are moving to and from feeding areas. Deer know that colder months are approaching. They eat more often to increase body fat during this period. The extra fat will keep them warm. The best place to shoot a deer is on trails that you discover while scouting before the season begins. During this time, deer still travel in groups. However, mature bucks slowly will break away from the herd as they become more aggressive toward other males.

THE RUT

The rut provides the most successful deer harvests. The rut is the best hunting period because bucks are constantly on the move in search of mating partners. The rut usually lasts for two weeks. You can tell when it is the rut by two signs. First, you will notice large rubs on the bases of smaller trees and circular scrapes on the ground. These are mating markings by bucks (male deer) and does (female deer), which give off scents to communicate with each other. These are good places to hunt because deer visit them so often during this period.

Second, during the rut, bucks follow their breeding instincts. They may travel several miles outside their normal range to seek new mates. Bucks let down their guard. They are more aggressive toward each other while competing for mates. They actually will engage in battle. Because they are always on the move,

Be extremely safety conscious during the rut, when many people are out hunting.

this is the chance for hunters to take a big buck at any hour of the day. Make sure that when you are hunting during this time you pay special attention to safety regulations. More hunters are in the woods now than at any other time. However, your chances of seeing deer are good, so you should hunt for as many hours as possible.

THE POSTRUT

During the postrut, deer are less active. At this point deer, especially larger bucks, do not like to move. They will have used up their energy during the rut. However, you might catch deer searching for food to rebuild their energy. It is also a chance to catch bucks or younger males that have not mated yet. But don't be surprised if you do not see any deer. During the postrut, whitetails move mostly at night.

Laws vary within states as to which sex of deer can be harvested. Most states also have regulated days set aside for harvesting does. Does often travel in large groups. They are seen more often than are male deer, so beginners should definitely take advantage of the opportunity to hunt these animals.

HUNTING SEASON

Hold on! Before you head out on the hunt, you have to make sure it is hunting season where you are. Hunting seasons are decided by each state. Different parts of a state have slightly different hunting seasons. In some places, bow hunters have separate hunting seasons. Some states also have laws that say which sex of deer you may hunt. In general, hunting seasons in the United States are in the fall. States set their hunting seasons around the rut period. Check with your local government to find out the hunting season in your area.

These two hunters have had a successful hunting outing.

33

TRACKING THE DEER

Regardless of during what time of year you hunt, there are certain guidelines that always apply. Hunting areas need to be approached from a downwind direction. Otherwise, a deer stands a better chance of smelling your scent. Always make sure you are downwind of the area in which you plan to spot deer. When moving through the woods, walk quietly and avoid making any loud noises such as snapping twigs or dropping an object. The most effective way to hunt deer is to sit still and wait patiently.

THE WAITING GAME

Hunters must use keen senses of hearing and sight to detect any noises or movements that might be made by a whitetail. Deer feed and move about at night. The best time to see them is early in the morning while they are returning to bedding areas. Another good

Hunters must look and listen carefully for signs of deer.

time is late in the afternoon when they are leaving their beds to feed. This is where experience becomes a factor. The more you hunt, the better you will learn the whitetail's movement patterns and behavior.

When you do spot a deer, do not get nervous. Remain calm, and wait for the animal to walk into effective range, where it presents a good shot. The ideal shot on a deer is directly behind its front shoulder. This will ensure a clean pass through the deer's most vital organs. Any shot outside this kill zone may only wound the deer or allow it to run several hundred yards before falling, two situations that you want to avoid. Use the same shooting methods that you practiced on the rifle range to make sure of a quick kill.

Moving into Position

If you are hunting on land, you may need to move into position before you fire your

Pay attention to a deer's body language. If its tail hangs down, the deer is relaxed. If its tail flares out, the deer may be getting ready to flee. If a deer stomps a front leg, bobs its head, or snorts, it sees something and is trying to get it to move; remain still.

weapon. The main rule to follow is to always move slowly. Plan your steps in advance. Look out for twigs or puddles that would make sounds. Then step while keeping your eyes up. Keep your eyes on your surroundings. Avoid moving through bright, sunny places. Try to move through shadowy spaces. This approach will make it harder for the deer to see you.

DEER CALLS

One way to attract deer is to copy their mating call. Have an experienced hunter teach you how to do a grunt call. If male deer hear a mating grunt, they think a doe is in the area. They will go to check out the situation. You also can try copying the sound of antlers hitting each other. If deer hear this sound, they think two deer are fighting over a doe. To make the sound of rattling antlers, you can knock two pieces of wood together. Better yet, if you have antlers from a previous kill, you can use them.

GETTING YOUR KILL

Once you have shot an animal, the next step is to retrieve it. If the shot has excellent placement, the animal may die instantly. Usually, however, the deer will run some distance, so tracking it is necessary. Try to always have another person help you in your search.

Take note of where the animal was hit, and carefully follow the blood trail. You may want to leave bits of toilet paper or ribbon to mark your direction.

When you locate your kill, you will need to transport it back home. Tie one end of a piece

Getting your kill back home can be half the battle!

of rope around the antlers or neck of the deer. Then wrap the rope one time around its muzzle. This method will keep the deer's head from getting tangled in brush as you pull.

You also must tag your deer. Tagging means that you must punch the day and month of the kill on the temporary tag and attach it to the animal's body. You will probably need to transport the deer to a tagging

and checking station. At the station, a permanent tag for the animal will be issued, as well as a new temporary tag for your next hunt.

ENJOY YOUR HUNT

Deer hunting is a challenging activity you can participate in with family and friends. It also is a great way to experience the outdoors and learn more about the natural world. As long as you follow all safety precautions and licensing requirements, you should have an enjoyable hunting experience. You may not always have a successful kill, but each time you hunt, you will be developing and improving your hunting skills. With practice, you will become more aware of deer behavior and become a better hunter.

Deer hunting can be an activity that your whole family can enjoy.

Safety Tips

- Always treat a gun as if it was loaded.
- Never point a weapon at another person.
- Always try to hunt with at least one partner.
- Always dress in layers and bring along a warm hat and gloves.
- Always tell someone where you are going and when you expect to return.
- Always wear blaze orange clothing, even if it is not required.
- Drink plenty of water and eat small snacks during your hunt.
- Keep all firearms pointed away from you with the safety switch on.
- Keep the safety on until you are ready to shoot, but do not assume the safety will prevent an accident!

- Do not mix guns with alcohol or drugs.
- Unload your weapon before climbing an object or if you are walking long distances.
- Don't climb into a tree stand with a loaded gun. Always pull it up after you.
- When hunting with other people, be aware of their exact movements and location.
- Never use a rifle scope for looking at objects. Use binoculars instead.
- Do not hoist a harvested deer over your shoulders. Always drag it with a rope.

New Words

bedding area a deer's sleeping area

bolt-action loaded with a hand-operated bolt

bow hunting a type of hunting in which a bow and arrow are used

buck a male deer that grows antlers of different sizes

buckshot a type of bullet

caliber indicates the size of a rifle barrel and which type of ammunition is required

camouflage a style of clothing that helps you blend into the woods

compound bow modern bow made of wood, fiberglass, and glue; it uses strings and pulleys to get more arrow speed

doe female deer

game animals hunted for sport or food

gauge barrel size; the number of lead balls that fit inside a rifle's barrel

harvest the act of shooting and recovering an animal

open-sighted having no scope

portable able to be carried or moved

postrut the period after rutting when deer are less active

prerut the period before rutting when deer travel constantly looking for food

rifle a type of firearm that has spiral grooves in its barrel to make bullets spin

rut period of time when bucks are trying to mate with does

safety a device on a firearm that keeps it from being fired

scope a device on a rifle that you look through to help you aim at targets far away

shotgun a type of firearm that has an ungrooved barrel and fires buckshot

tags tickets that are attached to an animal after it is harvested

tree stand man-made place in a tree where a hunter can sit and wait for deer

Resources

Scent-Lok

www.scentlok.com

This site teaches you the importance of eliminating scent from clothes when hunting. It also includes tips for remaining scent-free.

Whitetail Deer.Com

www.whitetaildeer.com

This site contains lots of information about the white-tailed deer. Get tips for deer hunting including safety information, weapons recommendations, and hunting conditions.

Whitetails Unlimited

www.whitetailsunlimited.org/index.asp

Learn about the whitetail, including information about their history, habitat, and food preference. This site also includes guidelines for deer hunting and firearm safety.

For Further Reading

Books
Evans, Sid. *The Deer Hunter's Almanac.* New York: Grove Atlantic, Incorporated, 1996.

Patent, Dorothy Hinshaw. *A Family Goes Hunting.* New York: Houghton Mifflin Company, 1991.

Smith, Richard P. *Deer Hunting.* Mechanicsburg, PA: Stackpole Books, 1991.

Weishuhn, Larry. *Southern Deer and Deer Hunting.* Iola, WI: Krause Publications, 1995.

Magazine
Bowhunter
6405 Flank Drive
Harrisburg, PA 17112
(800) 829-3340
Web site: *www.bowhunter.com*

Index

About the Author

Jonathan Ceaser is a lifelong deer hunter and fisherman living in Richmond, Virginia. Jonathan earned his B.A. at Virginia Tech.